MW01233350

Keto Diet For Women After 50 Secrets

An Effective Guide To Ketogenic Diet For Women Over 50 To Reset Your Metabolism & Stay Healthy With The Ketogenic Diet Meal Plan

Josephine Berg

© Copyright 2021 - All rights reserved.

The content contained within this book may not be reproduced, duplicated or transmitted without direct written permission from the author or the publisher.

Under no circumstances will any blame or legal responsibility be held against the publisher, or author, for any damages, reparation, or monetary loss due to the information contained within this book. Either directly or indirectly.

Legal Notice:

This book is copyright protected. This book is only for personal use. You cannot amend, distribute, sell, use, quote or paraphrase any part, or the content within this book, without the consent of the author or publisher.

Disclaimer Notice:

Please note the information contained within this document is for educational and entertainment purposes only. All effort has been executed to present accurate, up to date, and reliable, complete information. No warranties of any kind are declared or implied. Readers acknowledge that the author is not engaging in the rendering of legal, financial, medical or professional advice. The content within this book has been derived from various sources. Please consult a licensed professional before attempting any techniques outlined in this book.

By reading this document, the reader agrees that under no circumstances is the author responsible for any losses, direct or indirect, which are incurred as a result of the use of information contained within this document, including, but not limited to, errors, omissions, or inaccuracies.

TABLE OF CONTENTS

Introduction

When you use a ketogenic diet or lose a lot of weight, your body has to burn through its own fat stores to use as fuel. Over 50 studies show how healthy it is for weight loss, as well as many other health and performance advantages. Because it is recommended by many doctors, it is well-regarded.

As you decrease your carbohydrate intake, you can gain more fat as a greater percentage of your caloric intake is derived from protein on low carb. Being in a low-carb for anaerobic diet causes your body to have a metabolic state known as "ketosis," where fat from your own diet and fat from the rest of your diet is burned for energy.

The ketogenic diet is a quite low-carb, moderate-protein, high-fat diet, which is somewhat similar to the Atkins and the same as the paleo diet

It asks patients to drastically reduce carbohydrate intake and eat lots of fat instead. As you eliminate carbohydrates from your diet, your body enters into a metabolic state called ketosis, or fat metabolism.

When this occurs, your body uses fat as its primary source of energy, your fat oxidation rate skyrockets. When you eat a diet high in carbs, your liver also stores fat. The fat may supply energy for the brain, but if you get enough carbs from the diet to supply your daily needs (6Trusted Source, 7Trusted Source).

The extremely low carbohydrate content of the ketogenic diet may lead to massive reductions in blood sugar and insulin levels. These benefit stretches, such as improved energy, more energy ketones, and decreased inflammation, have many people flocking to the ketogenic diet.

Chapter-1

Is the Ketogenic Diet a Good Choice for Women Over 50?

In their younger adults, calorie expenditure slows by about 50 each day in order to maintain constant body weight.

Reduced exercise, as well as the risk of muscular breakdown and the ability to consume more calories due to a slowdown in metabolism, maybe a difficult to keep off as a constant weight.

A low-carb for women over 50

A few popular weight-loss methods in recent years include a low carbohydrate diet (keto) and fasting, but the keto diet has surged as a popular one recently.

We've received a lot of questions about whether or not following the diet is healthy and if it's doable in the long term.

What is the Ketogenic Diet?

Fasting, which helps the body use fat as a fuel, involves reducing the intake of carbs and increasing fat in the diet, so Keto is a way of increasing the body's fat-burning efficiency.

There is strong evidence to suggest that the ketogenic diet is beneficial for overall health and weight loss.

In particular, ketogenic diets have been successful at improving people's lipid metabolism without exacerbating food cravings that are commonly seen with other diets.

Other research has demonstrated that some people who have type 2 diabetes find that keto is helpful for controlling their symptoms.

That highlights the main principles of the ketogenic diet, which are that (1) fat should be the main source of fuel for the body instead of carbohydrates; (2) carbohydrates should be used as a quick energy source, such as sugar and glycogen stores; and (3) fats have an extremely high calorificaiter utility; and (4) a high calorificatiing diet creates metabolic waste.

The goal of the ketogenic diet is to use ketones for fuel

Lose weight and keep it off with Keto Over 50: An informative guide to implementing the ketogenic diet for women in their 50s

You're using a different fuel during extended periods of exertion, such as when you're exercising or long-distance running, because your body is using fatty acids or ketones instead of sugar.

Producing ketones occurs when you've managed to cut your carb intake and get the right amount of protein while eating a bit more carbs.

When you're eating keto-friendly foods that are digested by your body, your liver helps you to transfer fat into ketones, which can serve as an alternative source of energy for your whole body.

In order to be in ketosis, the body must be using fat as an energy source.

"Expand" is beneficial in some cases in expanding fat breakdown, thus enabling the body to use fat as fuel instead of its usual fuel source and resulting in the breakdown of unwanted fat tissue being more easily gotten rid of.

This method of fat loss not only helps you lose weight, but it helps to stabilize your energy levels and prevent your appetite from decreasing during the day.

The foods that will help you transition into and maintain a state of ketosis are composed of high amounts of omega-3 fatty acids from animal products like salmon, sardines, and herring and low amounts of carbohydrates and protein.

Keto diets work best for women who are over 50 years of age.

When people attempt to eat on the keto diet, it seems a lot more difficult because it's hard to figure out which food has high carbohydrates and which food has low carbohydrates, so it can be incorporated into a lot of people.

Here are a few great foods for women over 50 who are on the keto diet.

The Ultimate Guide to Weight Loss: this book goes beyond the keto basics and helps you put it all together to a keto diet complete food list of everything you should eat for weight loss.

processed meats as the primary source of protein, as well as leaner meats, as they are free of carbs

Fish and seafood, such as fried or breaded fish, are best avoided for the added carbohydrates.

Whether they are fried, poached, boiled, scrambled, or hard-boiled, you can have your eggs however you like; they're prepared.

veget richer, and food: those that grow in the ground gets less

Dairy: Choose dairy products that are high in fat; low-fat options are often sweetened with sugar.

Sources of nuts are good, but it is important to avoid eating too much, especially because they are high in fat

All berries are fine in moderation.

There are a lot of low-carb foods to choose from when following the ketogenic diet, and what you will find here are healthy options in most of the greatest quantity are dairy, meat, fish, cheese, bread, and eggs.

Sugar is the main enemy of insulin target

It's fine to have a little fruit as long as it doesn't add sugar to your diet.

Beers and alcoholic beverages: too many carbohydrates and sugars

The starches in this mix are equal to the number of refined carbohydrates found in white bread, rice, and pasta.

keto-fying your favorite foods

There may be some foods that you dislike that aren't suitable for people who have certain food allergies or sensitivities.

a keto-friendly plate made up of macadamia nuts, plain chicken breast, and unbuttered veggies

Giving yourself the ability to live outside of your comfort zone is always difficult.

Food and recipes have a way of being specific to our families that is difficult to leave behind, whether we want to or not and us.

So, When the type of foods you can't eat change, you can be able to restrict. Fortunately, you can get alternatives to the foods you can't eat, or they'll remain within the limits of keto.

This indicates that you can continue to eat sandwiches and pasta, which in my humble opinion is the best possible combination. This generally applies to a low GI food's long-term benefits: Generally, the best low GI foods should be chosen.

sugar-free bread is 20 times less carb than traditional bread

Not difficult to make, 2-ingreduce recipe

It only needs three ingredients to begin to simmer: rice, water, water, oil, and an open fire.

A cereal low-carb breakfast food

Can women over the age of 50 benefits from the Keto?

One thing you can be sure of with regard to Keto is that there are numerous factors to consider before determining whether or not it is suitable for you; however: It is completely up to you whether or not.

A low-carb for women over 5

As long as you are not afflicted with health problems, a ketogenic diet can be very good for you, especially for weight loss.

The most important thing to bear in mind is to eat a healthy balance of vegetables, proteins, low-fat dairy products, and unprocessed carbohydrates.

Just staying on a diet of whole foods is likely to be the most sustainable because it cuts costs less money and has less environmental impact.

It's important to remember that many studies indicate that attempts to track outcomes of the ketogenic diet aren't reliable. Avoid resorting to an unhealthy means of weight loss, such as fad diets or drastic lifestyle changes, and fasting. Instead, find a healthy eating approach that's good for you.

Just because something hasn't worked in the past doesn't mean it can't work in the future.

A low carbohydrate, high fat, moderate protein, and protein eating plan and diet plan can transform your body.

A ketogenic diet is a high-fat, moderate-protein, adequate-carbohydrate, and low-calorie meal plan, which consists of 75% fat, up to 20% protein, and 5% or fewer carbs in order to keep the protein and carbohydrate consumption within a fairly tight range while having plenty of micronutrients - the micronutrients (vitamins and minerals) needed.

At first, it may seem like you have to be difficult to give up carbohydrates, but it doesn't have to be in order to be done.

You should reduce the number of carbohydrates in your daily meals and snacks while simultaneously increasing the fat and protein content.

The more carbs that are consumed, the less likely the person is to be in a state of ketosis.

Carbs could affect everyone differently; some people may only get into ketosis if they eat at 20 grams per day, but others might require eating more to experience it.

Most people will find it to maintain a low-carbohydrate diet and nutritional ketosis if their carbohydrate intake is under 50% of their total daily calories.

Following a ketogenic diet means sticking to healthy food choices, and avoiding carbohydrate-rich options will lead to long-term weight loss for successful short-term goals.

Ketogenic food to consume

Meals and snacks should be comprised of these items: Fatty meats and higher amounts of vegetables (like avocados, butter, olive oil, olives, and olive oil) and lower amounts of carbohydrates, like bread and higher glycemic vegetables (like broccoli)

If you are concerned about nutritional benefits, you should focus on the production of pastured, organic whole eggs.

Poultry includes both chicken and turkey.

Omega-3 fatty fish: Freshly caught salmon, herring, and mackerel

Red meat: venison, pork, organ meats, and buffalo/bison from grass-fed cattle.

full-fat dairy: butter, full-fat yogurt, and heavy cream

Both red and low-fat, with cream cheese: full-fat cheese, cream cheese, mozzarella, and goat cheese; and goat cheese

These include Macadamia nuts, almonds, walnuts, peanut and sunflower seeds as well as all of these, also pumpkin seeds, ground sunflower seeds, and sesame.

Homemade nut butter, almond, cashew, and coconut butter are all suitable for use in this recipe.

These oils are excellent sources of beneficial fats: coconut oil, olive oil, avocado oil, and canola oil, and avocado oil, and sesame oil

While avocados can be incorporated into almost any dish or into snack food or meal mixtures of your choice

Other vegetables: Broccoli, tomatoes, mushrooms, and peppers (not in their starchy form).

These are commonly known as condiments: salt, pepper, vinegar, lemon juice, fresh herbs, and spices.

foods you should stay away from

A keto diet should not be followed while avoiding carb-rich foods

Some of the following foods should be avoided:

There are a number of different types of bread, baked goods, crackers, dough, and pastries on the menu here, and they're known by different names such as bread, white bread, and dough, as well as whole-wheat rolls.

Bitter things:caffeine: The casein from cow's milk, cocoas, orange juice, and maple sap are all sugar substitutes, but orange juice is more bitter.

Diluted sugar beverages: Soda, fruit juices, syrups, sports drinks, and tea.

Spaghetti, macaroni, and spaghetti.

Grains and other than wheat and rice and oats: Cereals, wheat- and oat-based breakfast foods

Also, starchy vegetables: Potatoes, sweet potatoes, corn, butternut squash, and peas, but these are not your best bets.

Beans and legumes: lentils are good; kidney beans, black beans, chickpeas, lentils are especially excellent.

Fruit: Oranges, pears, pineapples, bananas, and pineapples.

heavy or low-carb or high-carb sauces: barbecue sauce, sugary dressing, and dipping sauces

The list of possible ingredients that may increase a person's weight includes Alcoholic drinks (beer and colas), as well as sugary mixed drinks.

Though carbohydrates should be kept in moderation, low-type fruits such as berries may be consumed in limited amounts as long as you are in ketogenic macros [i.e.e. Carbohydrate-deficient but low in protein and fat].

Processed foods and unhealthy fats (for example, saturated, trans, and hydrogenated fats) can be harmful to your heart.

If you are not interested in meeting certain people or establishing relationships, certain topics or styles of conversation should be avoided:

damaging fats: Margarine, shortenings, and oils that are low in polyunsaturated fats, such as canola and corn oil.

Altered foods such as ready-to-to-eat and fast food, packaged meats, such as hot dogs, and lunch meats and lunch meats.

Artificial colors, preservatives, aspartame, and sweeteners such as sugar are added to these food products to extend their shelf life and make them more aesthetically pleasing, but their chemical components have been shown to lead to many diseases

sugar-free, rice, wheat, soy, and dairy beverages

sugar can be found in a variety of beverages, including juice,,, caffeinated, tea variety of beverages such as iced tea and soft drinks

While on a ketogenic diet, you must avoid high-carb foods just as you would any other carb-rich foods.

So we should cut our sugary beverages like Coke and Pepsi because of the health issues they may cause? It's no small that sugary drinks have been linked to various diseases, like obesity and diabetes?

It is wonderful that there are plenty of tasty, sugar-free diet alternatives for us on the keto diet.

Foods to drink on a low carbohydrate diet might include soft drinks and juices as well as full-fat milk, butter, heavy cream, bacon, and eggs.

WATER: Hydration is fundamental for both adults and children, and you should have it throughout the day.

Excellent soda alternative to carbonated water: Carbonated water has been shown to be a bit acidic and unhealthy; however, carbonated water can be made a lot more sparkly and attractive.

If you want to increase the flavor of your coffee, use heavy cream instead of milk.

Although the unfermented green tea leaves do provide some health benefits, the process of fermentation takes away from the very few that remain, making it not as delicious as unfermented green tea.

Chapter-2 Over 50 of Our Best Keto Recipes

For many people, new diets represent a new year's resolution. **The** ketogenic diet isn't simple (we've been discussing it for several years now), so if you're trying it for the first time, identifying the foods that are right for you is difficult. As a rule, your choices are usually low carb because that is where your body enters into a state of ketosis or to help your fat burn rather than using carbs for fuel. In order to be able to accomplish this, you must restrict your carbohydrates to about 20 grams of intake. It's not just about cutting carbs, as I like to emphasize; however, the diet is a little more highly adjusted. **P**rocessed foods and sugar are off the table and, and many people no longer eat much or any sweet fruits Alcohol can be enjoyed in moderation. A little dark chocolate can be beneficial, but it's preferable to avoid all dark chocolate as much as possible.

If you'd like to help you understand the potential confusions that arise from following a ketogenic diet, we want to assist you. There are well over 50 recipes in this collection that comply with the requirements of the rule of ketosis, regardless of what you're looking for in them to fit into ketosis. Breakfast through dinner will become a staple for you whether you stay on **a** diet or only for the month.

People who are new to the keto diet might think of bacon and eggs when they envision the typically get started out-of-of-the-the-the-the-box breakfast items, but these can be only the beginning of what you can eat in the morning. Other kinds of fruit, such as smoothies, pancakes, and even whole-grain bread**,** are included.

Return the foods and habits that are outside of the keto diet and lifestyle back into it

a stricter the diet, the fewer micronutrients by-like nutrients that you will be able to get from food. An extended regimen must be necessary to preserve the overall health or for those suffering from adrenal exhaustion or disease.

For the past month, Catherine has been doing a daily multivitamin supplement with Vitamin D and calcium but is now planning to try something different. When you're out working as hard as a mother, you want to ensure you're getting enough nutrients to keep your body running, at the very least. Catherine's daily micronutrients have been covered by her previously named vitamins and minerals.

Micronutrients are depleted by physical activity

A, B, C, magnesium, selenium, manganic acid, potassium, zinc, alpha-lipoic acid, or zinc/selenium, alpha-lipophilic acid

K-friendly diets deprive the body of micronutrients like B vitamins and magnesium

Stress depletes micronutrients such as vitamins, calcium, magnesium, and omega-3 fatty acids deplete both dietary and essential micronutrients.

This is only a partial list of micronutrients that can be used to illustrate the common denominators

We found that frequent training at high levels of training for an extended time both lead to elevated cortisol levels. Do a moderate volume of cycling that is below 75 minutes or a high-intensity cycle that lasts from 45 to 60 minutes to start, and then gradually increase your dosage to maximize cortisol release. a decrease in overall stress levels is critical for a woman who is training for long- or middle-distance running events

And if she gets more rest while training, she will have less stress.

She is tired and reporting problems with her energy levels. When someone is doing an endurance event, this is normal. It is also quite common for women trying to stay on keto after the age of 50 for long periods of time. It is difficult to maintain constant intensity while also listening to your body and enjoying frequent breaks. As a coach, I always want someone below their normal training level. When you're unsure, pause, the cause of fatigue could be either insufficient nutrients or an imbalance of hormones.

Non-nutritive, micronutrients, macronutrients, and macronutrients

her competition targets are reducing inflammation and optimizing her nutrient timing in order to allow her to have energy throughout training and racing. She works out in a very fast and exhausting manner in order to speed herself up the process of recovery for the next time she works out. Maintaining a healthy lean muscular and skeletal composition over the long term is one of her long-term goals.

Catherine might consider which micronutrients to increase because the results of the earlier study seem to indicate she has need of them:

Multivitamin consumed in multiple servings per day

Along with the other key nutrients, such as vitamin B, C, calcium, and Omega 3, appear to play a crucial role in healthy bone growth.

After physical activity, it is necessary to take a good amount of protein nutrition

Nutrition timing after physical activity for most older adults should be between 60 and 120 minutes. One problem: Since Catherine's training is becoming more frequent and intense, her post-exercise smoothie or high protein meal can be met sooner.

To prevent muscle loss, she should aim for 20-35 grams of protein, moderate-based carbohydrate consumption, and keep her carbs low; for reducing inflammation, she should get moderate levels of protein and low to moderate levels of carbs. If certain studies are applied, the findings suggest that older people can obtain similar results to younger people if they have twice the protein intake (40 gm compared to 20).

I like to have all of the ingredients in a blended recovery drink, but I don't always consume it. Including all of the other ingredients are shown to have anti-inflammatory properties

A high-fat, low-carbohydrate, moderate protein, very low-glycemic-index diet

A post-workout smoothie recipe that contains fruit juice and wheat grass-fed gelatin after intense training and cardio

2 quarts spinach2 liters

1/2/2 medium to half an avocado

with about 3/4 cup thawed frozen, pitted, and diced cherries

vegan (dairy-free) paleo and gluten-free, or plant-based protein

a cocoa powder made from cocoa beans (or nibs)

plain, unsweetened coconut milk

Talk to your level of fatigue about how frequently you are feeling it. If your training leaves you feeling fatigued and unable to rest, this may be a sign of overtraining.

A very high-fat, low carbohydrate, moderate protein, moderate-protein, or moderate-high protein diet will help you maintain ketosis while also encourages weight loss of fat.

Above all, whether you are exercising or preparing for a race, you must avoid the risk of developing adrenal fatigue. Following a specific and rigid training program increases the risk of adrenal exhaustion. Do pay attention to the volume of workouts according to your bodily needs; this can ensure that your work/training sessions are not so taxing that you cannot be performed with full strength.

Traditional methods of training for events may stress your body and your body, but giving your body proper nutrition has a high chance of improving your results significantly—or at least minimizing the amount of stress on your body—, is a lot of different.

(progressive) after six months of continual training, I have developed a workout plan that helped keep my cortisol in check and ensured my mass and body composition remained in balance while also enabling me to train progressively. Here is a way to find out about my plans.

Make sure you have a good level of strength training in your routine to prevent injury while also ensures bone retention from increased swimming and biking. They are both great for muscles and bone health, but unlike exercise, they don't provide the bone benefit of weight-bearing.

The best relaxation therapy

Find out how quickly you can go back to regular activities after your illness. If you answer these questions, then you will know how well your nutrition is going to work-outs are going to go. Recovery patterns that persist are typically indicate something long-term. They include constant aches and fatigue or an increase in how hard it is to perform daily activities.

To test your own heart rate, take a quick look in the mirror each morning when you'll Look for the changes in intensity, recovery after extended exercise sessions, rest days, and moderate ones. If your heart rate is consistently increased by 5 BPM over your normal training levels for more than three days, you should take it easy during the remainder of the week and try to get sufficient rest to recuperate and try the following week again.

You can also monitor the variability of the heart rate, which will show a difference between heartbeats.

Let's pretend you have a resting heart rate of 60 beats per minute. You might think that it's just a second long, but it is, in fact, between each beat. This is also an example of the law of diversification in practice: having a wide-ranging selection of heartbeats is ideal. The amount of time could be anywhere between .8 and 1.2 seconds, or perhaps a few smaller. Training may be unpredictable, but rest is not. A more predictable heart rate is better for day-to-to-day gains in aerobic capacity and thus for avoiding burnout.

You need to use special equipment, plus an app, in order to view this content. Both products are consumed first thing in the morning. Use the resting heart rate as a baseline and compare it to a patient's rate before and after treatment.

Finally, one could purchase Sleep Number SleepIQ monitors, which can track your number of hours of sleep per night, allowing one to get a more detailed look at your health and well-being. I prefer it to a device which I can wear. R resting heart rate, HRV, and your sleep duration can help you determine how well you're resting and how you'll benefit from training. A sense of fatigue is important, and finding ways to work around it will help. But if that's a regular occurrence, and if it builds up over time, seek new training balance by doing something else for a while.

Breakfast Recipes

1. Sausage Breakfast

Macros: Fat 76% | Protein 22% | Carbs 2%

Prep time: 10 minutes | Cook time: 50 minutes | Serves 8

T he sausage breakfast is filled with a delicious egg mixture over a

crescent crust. The meal is easy to prepare and takes a short time

to cook.

2 tablespoons olive oil, divided 1 pound (454 g) homemade sausage

8 large eggs 1 tablespoon fresh oregano, chopped

2 cups cooked spaghetti squash Sea salt and ground black pepper to

taste ½ cup Cheddar cheese, shredded

1. Preheat the oven to 375°F (190°C) and grease a casserole dish

    with 1 tablespoon of olive oil.

2. Heat the remaining olive oil in a skillet. Add the sausages and

    cook for 5 minutes or until they are browned.

3. In a bowl, break the eggs and whisk well. Add oregano and squash, then mix well. Add salt and pepper to season. Add the sausage, then stir to mix.

4. Pour the sausage mixture in the casserole dish.

5. Scatter the cheese over the mixture and cover loosely with an aluminum foil.

6. Bake in the preheated oven for about 30 minutes. Remove the aluminum foil, then bake for 15 minutes more.

7. Allow the casserole to cool for about 8 minutes before serving.

STORAGE: Store in an airtight container in the fridge for up to 4 days or in the freezer for up to 1 month.

REHEAT: Microwave, covered, until it reaches the desired temperature.

SERVE IT WITH: To make this a complete meal, serve with chocolate peanut butter smoothie.

PER SERVING

calories: 297 | fat: 25.0g | total carbs: 4.0g | fiber: 2.0g | protein: 18.0g

2. Chicken And Egg Stuffed Avocado

Macros: Fat 71% | Protein 24% | Carbs 5%

Prep time: 10 minutes | Cook time: 20 minutes | Serves 4

A vocado and chicken blend in well in eggs. Salt and pepper add

spice to the dish. The meal is perfect for breakfast.

2 peeled and pitted avocados, halved lengthwise

4 eggs

1 (4-ounce / 113-g) cooked chicken breast, shredded

¼ cup Cheddar cheese, shredded

Sea salt and freshly ground black pepper, to taste

1. Preheat the oven to 425°F (220°C).

2. Double the size of the hole in each avocado half with a spoon

   and arrange on a baking dish, hollow parts facing up.

3. In every hole, crack an egg and divide the chicken breast

   between every half of the avocado. Sprinkle with the Cheddar

   cheese and add salt and pepper to season.

4. Bake for about 20 minutes or until the eggs are cooked through.

5. Transfer to four serving plates and serve while warm.

STORAGE: Store in an airtight container in the fridge for up to 4 days or in the freezer for up to 1 month.

REHEAT: Microwave, covered, until it reaches the desired temperature.

SERVE IT WITH: To make this a complete meal, serve with strawberry zucchini chia smoothie.

PER SERVING

calories: 330 | fat: 26.0g | total carbs: 8.0g | fiber: 4.0g | protein: 20.0g

3. Bacon And Broccoli Egg Muffins

Macros: Fat 66% | Protein 31% | Carbs 3%

Prep time: 20 minutes | Cook time: 15 minutes | Serves 3

T he broccoli egg muffins are packed with protein and low net carb which provides a healthy diet. The meal is recommended for breakfast because it sustains your energy for the whole day.

1 cup broccoli, chopped 3 slices bacon 6 beaten eggs

½ teaspoon black pepper, ground ¼ teaspoon garlic powder ½ teaspoon salt A few drops of Sriracha hot sauce

1 cup Cheddar cheese, shredded

SPECIAL EQUIPMENT:

A 6-cup muffin pan

1. Preheat the oven to 350°F (180°C) and line 6 cups of muffin pan with silicone liners. Set aside.

2. Boil the broccoli in a pot of water for 6 to 8 minutes or until tender, then chop into ¼-inch pieces. Set aside.

3. In a nonstick skillet, fry the slices of bacon for about 8 minutes until crispy, then lay on a paper towel to drain.

4. In a bowl, pour the beaten eggs. Add pepper, garlic, hot sauce, and salt. Whisk well to mix.

5. Put the broccoli into the muffin cups. Top with the bacon, Cheddar cheese, and the egg mixture.

6. Bake in the preheated oven for 25 minutes or until eggs are set.

7. Transfer to serving plates to cool before serving.

STORAGE: Store in an airtight container in the fridge for up to 4 days or in the freezer for up to 1 month.

REHEAT: Microwave, covered, until it reaches the desired temperature.

SERVE IT WITH: To make this a complete meal, serve with coconut blackberry mint smoothie.

PER SERVING

calories: 296 | fat: 21.6g | total carbs: 6.5g | fiber: 4.0g | protein: 23.0g

4. Scrambled Eggs with Cheese And Chili

Macros: Fat 68% | Protein 29% | Carbs 3%

Prep time: 5 minutes | Cook time: 5 minutes | Serves 2

T he scrambled eggs with chili is a magnificent way to start the

day, they're packed with flavor and contain nutrients that offer a

hearty southern breakfast. The best part is they take a short time

to prepare.

4 large eggs

1½ teaspoons butter, unsalted

½ cup warm homemade chili

Salt and ground black pepper, to taste

½ sliced avocado

¼ cup sour cream

¼ cup Cheddar cheese, shredded

1. Whisk the eggs in a bowl.

2. In a skillet, add the butter and heat to melt. Add the eggs then sauté until scrambled. Add the chili, then stir to mix.

3. Add salt and pepper to season.

4. Transfer to serving plates and serve with avocado, sour cream, and cheese.

STORAGE: Store in an airtight container in the fridge for up to 4 days or in the freezer for up to 1 month.

REHEAT: Microwave, covered, until it reaches the desired temperature.

SERVE IT WITH: To make this a complete meal, serve with cinnamon raspberry breakfast smoothie.

PER SERVING

calories: 496| fat: 37.6g | total carbs: 8.2g | fiber: 4.0g | protein: 35.3g

Appetizers and Snacks

5. Buttered   Coconut Puffs

Macros: Fat 87% | Protein 10% | Carbs 3%

Prep time: 0 minutes | Cook time: 40 minutes | Serves 2

I t has simple ingredients that can be prepared in no time. They

are basic and sweet. The meal is versatile as it can complement a

number of different foods. It can be taken as breakfast or dinner.

1 tablespoon olive oil, for greasing the cookie sheet

¼ cup butter

½ cup water

½ cup coconut flour

2 eggs

A handful of spiced fennel, for filling

1. Preheat the oven to 375ºF (190ºC) and grease the cookie sheet

    with olive oil. Set aside.

2. Heat the butter and water in a saucepan over medium heat until the butter melts. Pour the flour into the saucepan all at once. Vigorously stir until it forms a ball in the middle of the pan. Set aside.

3. Add the eggs, one at a time, then beat the mixture until fully blended and stiff. Drop about ¾ teaspoon portions onto the cookie sheet. Gently smooth the pointed peaks with a moistened finger, and round the tops to ensure even rising.

4. Bake for about 40 minutes until puffs rise and are golden brown on top. Transfer to a wire rack to cool completely.

5. Slit an opening on one side, then stuff with the filling before serving.

STORAGE: Store in an airtight container in the fridge for up to 3 days.

SERVE IT WITH: To add more flavors to this meal, you can serve sprinkled with coconut flakes.

PER SERVING

calories: 404 | fat: 39.5g | total carbs: 3.3g | fiber: 0.7g | protein: 9.6g

6. Baked Beef, Pork and Veal Meatballs

Macros: Fat 74% | Protein 24% | Carbs 2%

Prep time: 30 minutes | Cook time: 30 minutes | Serves 8

T he combination of the beef, veal, and pork sound perfect, right?

The mixture makes the meal very delicious. A perfect snack for all times.

1 pound (454 g) ground beef

½ pound (227 g) ground pork

½ pound (227 g) ground veal

1 cup freshly grated Romano cheese, plus more Romano for garnish

2 minced cloves garlic

2 eggs, whisked

Salt and ground black pepper, to taste

1½ tablespoons chopped Italian flat leaf parsley

2 cups shredded coconut

1½ cups lukewarm water

1 cup olive oil

1. In a large bowl, add the beef, pork, and veal. Stir to mix well. Add the cheese, whisked eggs, garlic, pepper, salt, and parsley. Blend well.

2. Add the coconut, then slowly add ½ cup water as you stir until the mixture is moist but still able to hold its shape when rolled into meatballs. Form the mixture into 2-inch meatballs with your wet hands.

3. In a nonstick skillet, heat the olive oil, then fry the meatballs for about 15 minutes (in batches), turning occasionally, until evenly browned and slightly crispy.

4. Remove from the heat and sprinkle with Romano cheese on top for garnish, if desired.

STORAGE: Store in an airtight container in the fridge for up to 4 days or in the freezer for up to 1 month.

REHEAT: Microwave, covered, until the desired temperature is reached or reheat in a frying pan or air fryer / instant pot, covered, on medium.

SERVE IT WITH: To make this a complete meal, serve with Turmeric Beef Bone Broth.

PER SERVING

calories: 591 | fat: 49g | total carbs: 3.2g | fiber: 0.7g | protein: 33.1g

7. Stuffed Cheesy Mushrooms

Macros: Fat 76% | Protein 9% | Carbs 16%

Prep time: 25 minutes | Cook time: 20 minutes | Serves 3

A re you a mushroom lover? This is a delicious meal tailored just

for you. The meal can turn to be your favorite as it is rich in flavors.

It is a keto-friendly meal you will always enjoy.

12 whole fresh mushrooms

1 tablespoon olive oil

1 tablespoon minced garlic

1 (8-ounce / 227-g) package softened cream cheese

¼ teaspoon ground cayenne pepper

¼ teaspoon ground black pepper

¼ teaspoon onion powder

¼ cup grated Parmesan cheese

Cooking spray

1. Preheat the oven to 350ºF (180ºC) and spray a baking sheet with cooking spray. Set aside.

2. On a flat work surface, remove the mushroom stems, and finely chop them as you discard the tough stem endings. Reserve the mushroom caps on a plate.

3. In a nonstick skillet, heat the olive oil over medium heat. Add the chopped mushroom stems and garlic. Fry them until all the moisture disappears, then transfer to a bowl to cool for 5 minutes.

4. Add the cream cheese, cayenne pepper, black pepper, onion powder and Parmesan cheese into the bowl of mushroom mixture. Stir thoroughly until well combined.

5. Using a spoon, stuff every mushroom cap with a considerable amount of the filling, then arrange the stuffed mushroom caps on the baking sheet.

6. Bake for about 20 minutes until the liquid starts to form under the caps and caps are piping hot.

7. Remove from the oven and serve warm on a plate.

STORAGE: Store in an airtight container in the fridge for up to 3 days.

REHEAT: Microwave, covered, until it reaches the desired temperature.

SERVE IT WITH: To make this a complete meal, serve with fresh salad greens or a side dish of your choice.

PER SERVING

calories: 361 | fat: 29.9g | total carbs: 16.6g | fiber: 2.0g | protein: 9.8g

8. Grilled Spicy Shrimp

Macros: Fat 75% | Protein 22% | Carbs 3%

Prep time: 30 minutes | Cook time: 10 minutes | Serves 6

T his is a great recipe to enjoy. The oregano adds color and taste to the food. It takes a few minutes to cook. It is also spicy because of the hot pepper sauce.

1 cup plus 1 tablespoon olive oil

1 juiced lemon

¼ cup chopped fresh parsley

3 minced cloves garlic

2 tablespoons hot pepper sauce

2 teaspoons dried oregano

1 teaspoon ground black pepper

1 teaspoon salt

2 pounds (907 g) peeled and deveined large shrimp, tail-on

SPECIAL EQUIPMENT:

6 bamboo skewers (about 10 inches (25 cm) long), soaked for at least 30 minutes

1. Make the marinade: Combine 1 cup of olive oil, lemon juice, parsley, garlic, hot sauce, oregano, black pepper, and salt in a bowl. Stir well to incorporate.

2. Reserve some of the marinade for basting in a separate bowl. Pour the remaining marinade into a resealable plastic bag containing the shrimp. Shake and seal the bag, then transfer to the refrigerator and marinate for approximately 2 hours.

3. Preheat the grill to medium-low heat.

4. Thread the marinated shrimp onto the skewers, then discard the marinade.

5. Slightly oil the grill grates with 1 tablespoon of olive oil, then grill each side of the shrimp for about 5 minutes until the flesh is totally pink and opaque, basting frequently with the marinade you have reserved.

6. Cool for 5 minutes before serving.

STORAGE: Store in an airtight container in the fridge for up to 4 days or in the freezer for up to 1 month.

REHEAT: Microwave, covered, until it reaches the desired temperature.

SERVE IT WITH: To make this a complete meal, enjoy the grilled shrimp on a bed of greens.

PER SERVING

calories: 436 | fat: 37.6g | total carbs: 3.9g | fiber: 0.6g | protein: 21.0g

9. Almond Sausage Balls

Macros: Fat 74% | Proteins 19% | Carbs 7%

Prep time: 30 minutes | Cook time: 25 minutes | Serves 6

W ith only five ingredients, get into the kitchen and prepare

almond sausage balls within a few minutes. Take the keto balls

anytime you feel hungry. Prepare in advance to save time. If you

have kids, do not miss out on these tasty balls.

 1 cup almond flour, blanched

3 ounces bulk Italian sausage

1¼ cups sharp Cheddar cheese, shredded

2 teaspoons baking powder

1 large egg

1. Start by preheating the oven to 350ºF (180ºC) then grease a
   baking tray.

2. In a mixing bowl, mix the almond flour, Italian sausage, Cheddar
   cheese, baking powder, and the egg until mixed evenly.

3. Make equal-sized balls out of the mixture, then put them on the baking tray.

4. Put in the oven and bake for 20 minutes or until golden brown.

5. Remove from the oven and serve.

STORAGE: Store in an airtight container in the fridge for up to 1 week.

REHEAT: Microwave, covered, until it reaches the desired temperature.

PER SERVING

calories: 266 | fat: 22.5g | total carbs: 4.7g | fiber: 2.0g | protein: 13.0g

10.Cheesy Keto Cupcakes

Macros: Fat 85% | Proteins 9% | Carbs 6%

Prep time: 10 minutes | Cook: 20 minutes | Serves 12

It requires few ingredients when preparing this recipe. Only six ingredients and you have your cupcakes ready. They are soft, tasty and delicious. Good, especially for kids.

¼ cup melted butter   ½ cup   almond meal   teaspoon vanilla extract 2 (8-ounce / 227-g) packages cream cheese, softened

¾ cup Swerve 2 beaten eggs

SPECIAL EQUIPMENT:

A 12-cup

1. Start by preheating the oven at 350ºF (180ºC) then line a muffin pan with 12 paper liners.

2. In a mixing bowl, mix the butter and almond meal until smooth, then spoon the mixture into the bottom of the muffin cups. Press into a flat crust.

3. In a mixing bowl, combine vanilla extract, cream cheese, Swerve, and eggs.

4. Set the electric mixer to medium, then beat the mixture until smooth.

5. Spoon the mixture on top of the muffin cups.

6. Bake in the oven until the cream cheese is nearly set in the middle, for about 17 minutes.

7. Remove from the oven and let the cupcakes cool.

8. Once cooled, refrigerate for 8 hours to overnight before serving.

STORAGE: Store in an airtight container in the fridge for up to 1 days or in the freezer for up to 1 month.

REHEAT: Microwave, covered, until the desired temperature is reached or reheat in a frying pan or air fryer / instant pot, covered, on medium.

PER SERVING

calories: 169 | fat: 16.0g | total carbs: 2.7g | fiber: 0g | protein: 3.8g

Dinner Recipes

11.Juicy Beef Cheeseburgers

Preparation Time **: 10 minutes**

Cooking Time :20 minutes

Servings **: 6**

Ingredients

- 1 pound ground beef ½ cup green onions, chopped

- 2 garlic cloves, finely chopped ¼ tsp black pepper

- Salt and cayenne pepper, to taste 2 oz mascarpone cheese

- 3 oz pecorino Romano cheese, grated

- **2 tbsp olive oil**

Directions

1. In a mixing bowl, mix ground beef, garlic, cayenne pepper, black pepper, green onions, and salt. Shape into 6 balls; then flatten to make burgers.

2. In a separate bowl, mix mascarpone with grated pecorino Romano cheeses. Split the cheese mixture among prepared patties.

3. Wrap the meat mixture around the cheese mixture to ensure that the filling is sealed inside. Warm oil in a skillet over medium heat.

4. **Cook the burgers for 5 minutes each side.**

Nutrition:

- Calories 130

- Total Fats 8g

- Carbs: 5g

- Protein 16g

- Dietary Fiber: 2g

12.Zucchini with Blue Cheese and Walnuts

Preparation Time **: 10 minutes**

Cooking Time: **60 minutes**

Servings **: 6**

Ingredients

- 2 tbsp olive oil

- 6 zucchinis, sliced

- 1 ⅓ cups heavy cream

- 1 cup sour cream

- 8 ounces blue cheese

- 1 tsp Italian seasoning

- **¼ cup walnut halves**

Directions

1. Set a grill pan over medium heat. Season zucchinis with Italian seasoning and drizzle with olive oil. Grill the

zucchini until lightly charred. Remove to a serving platter.

2. In a dry pan over medium heat, toast the walnuts for 2-3 minutes and set aside.

3. Add the heavy cream, blue cheese, and sour cream to the pan and mix until everything is well combined.

4. **Let cool for a few minutes and scatter over the grilled zucchini. Top with walnuts to serve.**

Nutrition:

- Calories 181

- Total Fats 11.5g

- Carbs: 1.8g

- Protein 27.3g

- Dietary Fiber: 0.7g

Easy Peasy Recipes

13.Cauliflower Pizza with Salami

<u>Ingredients</u> for 4 servings

4 oz salami slices

1 tbsp dried thyme

2 cups grated mozzarella

¼ cup tomato sauce

4 cups cauliflower rice

<u>Instructions - Total Time</u>: around 40 minutes

Preheat oven to 370 F. Microwave cauliflower rice mixed with 1 tbsp of water for 1 minute. Remove and mix in 1 cup of the mozzarella and thyme. Pour the mixture into a greased baking dish, spread out and bake for 5 minutes. Remove the dish and spread the tomato sauce on top. Scatter the remaining mozzarella on the sauce and then arrange salami slices on top. Bake for 15 minutes.

Per serving: Cal 281; Net Carbs 2g; Fats 15g; Protein 20g

14. Broccoli Crust Pizza Margherita

Ingredients for 2 servings

2 ½ oz cremini mushrooms, sliced   6 tbsp tomato sauce

4 eggs   1 small red onion, sliced

1 small head broccoli, riced   ½ cup cottage cheese

¼ cup shredded cheddar   ½ tbsp olive oil

¼ cup Parmesan cheese   A handful of fresh basil

½ tsp Italian seasoning   Salt and black pepper to taste

Instructions - Total Time: around 40 minutes

Preheat oven to 380 F. Line a baking sheet with wax paper.

Microwave broccoli for 2 minutes; let cool. Crack in the eggs, add cheeses, salt, pepper, and Italian seasoning and whisk until combined. Spread the mixture on the baking sheet and bake for 15 minutes. Allow cooling the crust for 2 minutes. Spread tomato sauce on the crust, scatter with mushrooms, onion, and cottage cheese; drizzle with olive oil. Place the pan in the oven to bake for 15 minutes.

Scatter with basil leaves, slice, and serve.

Per serving: Cal 289; Net Carbs 0.8g; Fat 19g; Protein 13g

15.Zoodles al Pesto

Ingredients for 4 servings

28 oz tofu, pressed and cubed

2/3 cup grated Pecorino Romano cheese

1 red bell pepper, sliced

6 zucchinis, spiralized

¼ cup basil pesto

1 white onion, chopped

½ cup shredded mozzarella

2 tbsp olive oil

Toasted pine nuts to garnish

1 garlic clove, minced

Salt and black pepper to taste

Instructions - Total Time: around 20 minutes

Warm olive oil in a pot and sauté onion and garlic for 3 minutes. Add in tofu and cook until golden on all sides, then pour in the bell pepper and cook for 4 minutes. Mix in zucchini, pour pesto on top, and season with salt and pepper. Cook for 3-4 minutes. Stir in the Pecorino cheese. Top with mozzarella and garnish with pine nuts.

Per serving: Cal 481; Net Carbs 5.4g; Fat 32g; Protein 20g

16.Chia & Blackberry Pudding

Ingredients for 4 servings

½ cup Greek yogurt   1 tsp vanilla extract

1 cup fresh blackberries   7 tbsp chia seeds

1 ½ cups coconut milk   3 tbsp chopped almonds

4 tsp sugar-free maple syrup   Mint leaves to garnish

Instructions - Total Time: around 45 minutes

Place the coconut milk, Greek yogurt, maple syrup, and vanilla extract in a bowl and stir until evenly combined. Mix in the chia seeds. Puree half of the blackberries in a bowl using a fork and stir in the yogurt mixture. Share the mixture into medium mason jars, cover the lids and refrigerate for 30 minutes to thicken the pudding. Remove the jars, take off the lid, and stir the mixture. Garnish with the remaining blackberries, almonds, and some mint leaves. Serve and enjoy!.

Per serving: Cal 299; Net Carbs 6.3g; Fat 23g; Protein 7g

17.Balsamic Strawberry Pizza

Ingredients for 4 servings

2 tbsp cream cheese, softened	1 celery stalk, chopped
3 cups shredded mozzarella	1 tomato, chopped
1 tbsp olive oil	2 tbsp balsamic vinegar
¾ cup almond flour	1 cup strawberries, halved
2 tbsp almond meal	1 tbsp chopped mint leaves

Instructions - Total Time: around 35 minutes

- Preheat oven to 390 F. Line a pizza pan with parchment paper. Microwave 2 cups of mozzarella cheese and cream cheese for 1 minute.

- Remove and mix in almond flour and almond meal. Spread the mixture on the pizza pan

- bake for 10 minutes. Spread remaining mozzarella cheese on the crust. In a bowl, toss celery, tomato, olive oil, and balsamic vinegar. Spoon the mixture onto the mozzarella cheese and arrange the strawberries on top.

Top with mint leaves. Bake for 15 minutes. Serve sliced.

Per serving: Cal 312; Net Carbs 4g; Fats 11g; Protein 28g

Salads & Soups Recipes

18.Cheddar & Turkey Meatball Sala d

Ingredients for 4 servings

3 tbsp olive oil

1 tbsp lemon juice

1 lb ground turkey

Salt and black pepper to taste

1 head romaine lettuce, torn

2 tomatoes, sliced

¼ red onion, sliced

3 oz yellow cheddar, shredde d

Directions and Total Time: approx. 30 minutes

Mix the ground turkey with salt and black pepper and shape into meatballs. Refrigerate for 10 minutes.

Heat half of the olive oil in a pan over medium heat. Fry the meatballs on all sides for 10 minutes until browned and cooked within. Transfer to a wire rack to drain oil. Mix the lettuce, tomatoes, and red onion in a salad bowl, season with the remaining olive oil, salt, lemon juice, and pepper. Toss and add the meatballs on top. Scatter the cheese over the salad and serve.

Per serving: Cal 312; Fat 22g; Net Carbs 1.9g; Protein 19g

19.Warm Cauliflower Sala d

Ingredients **for 4 servings**

1 cup roasted bell peppers, chopped

2 tbsp celery leaves, chopped

10 oz cauliflower florets

1 red onion, sliced

¼ cup extra-virgin olive oil

1 tbsp wine vinegar

1 tsp yellow mustard

Salt and black pepper, to taste

½ cup black olives, chopped ½ cup cashew nuts

Directions **and Total Time: approx. 15 minutes**

Steam cauliflower in salted water in a pot over medium heat for

5 minutes; drain and transfer to a salad bowl. Add in roasted

peppers, olives, and red onion.

In a small dish, combine salt, olive oil, mustard, black pepper, and vinegar. Sprinkle the mixture over the veggies. Top with cashew nuts and celery and serve.

Per serving: Cal 213; Fat 16g; Net Carbs 7.4g; Protein 5.2g

20.Arugula & Roasted Pepper Sala d

Ingredients **for 4 servings**

2 lb red bell peppers, deseeded and cut into wedges

1/3 cup arugula

½ cup Kalamata olives, pitted

3 tbsp chopped walnuts

½ tsp Swerve sugar

2 tbsp olive oil

1 tbsp mint leaves

½ tbsp balsamic vinegar ¼ cup crumbled goat cheese

Toasted pine nuts for topping Salt and black pepper to taste

Directions **and Total Time: approx. 30 minutes**

Preheat oven to 400 F. Pour bell peppers on a roasting pan; season with Swerve sugar and drizzle with half of the olive oil. Roast for 20 minutes or until slightly charred; set aside to cool.

Put arugula in a salad bowl and scatter with roasted bell peppers, olives, mint, walnuts, and drizzle with vinegar and olive oil. Season with salt and pepper. Toss and top with goat cheese and pine nuts.

Per serving: Cal 159; Net Carbs 4.3g; Fat 13g; Protein 3.3g

21.Smoked Salmon Sala d

<u>Ingredients</u> **for 2 servings**

2 slices smoked salmon, chopped

1 tsp onion flakes 3 tbsp mayonnaise

½ Romaine lettuce, shredded 1 tbsp lime juice

1 tbsp extra virgin olive oil Sea salt to taste

½ avocado, sliced

<u>Directions</u> **and Total Time: approx. 10 minutes**

Combine the salmon, mayonnaise, lime juice, olive oil, and salt in a bowl; mix to combine. On a salad platter, arrange the shredded lettuce and onion flakes. Spread the salmon mixture over and top with avocado slices.

Per serving: Cal 231; Fat 20g; Net Carbs 2.2g; Protein 8.5g

22.Greek Beef Meatball Sala d

Ingredients **for 4 servings**

2 tbsp almond milk

1 lb ground beef

1 onion, grated

¼ cup pork rinds, crushed

1 egg, whisked

1 tbsp fresh parsley, chopped

Salt and black pepper, to taste

1 garlic clove, minced

1 tbsp fresh mint, chopped

½ tsp dried oregano

4 tbsp olive oil

1 cup cherry tomatoes, halved

1 Lebanese cucumber, sliced

1 cup butterhead lettuce, torn

1½ tbsp lemon juice

1 cup Greek yogurt

<u>Directions</u> and Total Time: approx. 20 minutes

In a bowl, mix the almond milk, ground beef, salt, onion, parsley, black pepper, egg, pork rinds, oregano, and garlic. Roll the mixture into balls. Warm half of the oil in a pan over medium heat and fry the meatballs for 8-10 minutes. Remove to a paper towel–lined plate to drain.

In a salad plate, combine lettuce, cherry tomatoes, and cucumber. Mix in the remaining oil, lemon juice, black pepper, and salt. Whisk the yogurt with mint and spread it over the salad; top with meatballs to serve.

Per serving: Cal 488; Fat 31g; Net Carbs 6.3g; Protein 42g

23.Caprese Salad Stacks with Anchovie s

Ingredients **for 4 servings**

4 anchovy fillets in oil

12 fresh mozzarella slices

4 red tomato slices

4 yellow tomato slices

1 cup basil pesto

Directions **and Total Time: approx. 10 minutes**

Take a serving platter and alternately stack a tomato slice, a mozzarella slice, a yellow tomato slice, another mozzarella slice, a red tomato slice, and then a mozzarella slice on it. Repeat making 3 more stacks in the same way. Spoon pesto all over. Arrange anchovies on top and serve.

Per serving: Cal 182; Net Carbs 3.5g; Fat 6g; Protein 17g

Poultry Recipes

24.Grilled Chicken Breast

Macros: Fat 34% | Protein 65% | Carbs 1%

Prep time: 15 minutes | Cook time: 20 minutes | Serves 4

I f you are craving for some juicy grilled chicken while on keto diet

then this grilled chicken breast is the best option. You can prepare

this recipe for lunch or dinner and enjoy with your family.

1 tablespoon olive oil

1 teaspoon steak sauce

2 tablespoons keto-friendly mayonnaise

⅓ teaspoon liquid stevia

⅓ cup Dijon mustard

4 skinless, boneless chicken breast halves

1. Start by preheating the grill on medium heat and lightly grease

   the grill grate with olive oil.

2. Mix together the steak sauce, mayonnaise, stevia, and mustard in a bowl. Reserve some mustard sauce for basting in another bowl, then coat the chicken with the remaining sauce.

3. Grill the chicken for about 20 minutes until the juices are clear, flipping occasionally and basting frequently with the reserved sauce.

4. Remove from the grill and serve hot.

STORAGE: Store in an airtight container in the fridge for up to 1 week

REHEAT: Microwave, covered, until the desired temperature is reached or reheat in a frying pan or air fryer / instant pot, covered, on medium.

SERVE IT WITH: To make this a complete meal, serve the grilled chicken with creamy spinach dill.

PER SERVING

calories: 333 | fat: 12.6g | total carbs: 1.5g | fiber: 0.9g | protein: 54.3g

25.Bacon-Wrapped Chicken Breasts Stuffed With Spinach

Macros: Fat 59% | Protein 39% | Carbs 2%

Prep time: 25 minutes | Cook time: 1 hour | Serves 4

T rust me, this easy bacon-wrapped chicken breasts stuffed with

spinach will become your family favorite! The flavor of the cheeses

will bring you and your families tons of flavor. And the choice of

spinach for this recipe will also increase the nutritional value of the

meal.

1 (10-ounce / 284-g) package frozen chopped spinach, thawed and

drained

½ cup mayonnaise, keto-friendly

½ cup feta cheese, shredded

2 cloves garlic, chopped

4 skinless, boneless chicken breasts

4 slices bacon

1. Preheat the oven to 375ºF (190ºC).

2. Combine the spinach, mayo, feta cheese, and garlic in a bowl, then set aside.

3. Cut the chicken crosswise to butterfly the chicken breasts, (butterfly cutting technique: not to cut the chicken breast through, leave a 1-inch space uncut at the end of the chicken. So when flipping open the halved chicken breast, it resembles a butterfly.)

4. Unfold the chicken breasts like a book. Divide and arrange the spinach mixture over each breast, then wrap each breast with a slice of bacon and secure with a toothpick.

5. Arrange them in a baking dish, and cover a piece of aluminum foil. Place the dish in the preheated oven and bake for 1 hour or until the bacon is crispy and the juice of chicken breasts run clear.

6. Remove the baking dish from the oven and serve warm.

STORAGE: Store in an airtight container in the fridge for up to 4 days or in the freezer for up to 1 month.

REHEAT: Microwave, covered, until the desired temperature is reached or reheat in a frying pan or air fryer / instant pot, covered, on medium.

SERVE IT WITH: To make this a complete meal, serve them on a bed of greens or serve with a cherry tomato and zucchini salad.

PER SERVING

calories: 626 | fat: 41.3g | total carbs: 3.7g | fiber: 1.4g | protein: 61.2g

26.Rotisserie-Style Roast Chicken

Macros: Fat 64% | Protein 35% | Carbs 1%

Prep time:10minutes | Cook time: 5 hours | Serves 8

W ith minimal preparation and about 5 hours' cooking time,you

can get that restaurant-style rotisserie chicken at home as you ever

wish. It is super simple to make. No special skills are required. It is

delicious and the leftovers are just as good the next day!

1 teaspoon onion powder

1 teaspoon white pepper

1 teaspoon dried thyme

½ teaspoon garlic powder

½ teaspoon cayenne pepper

1 teaspoons paprika

2 teaspoons salt

½ teaspoon black pepper

1 (4-pound / 1.8-kg) whole chickens, giblets removed, rinsed and pat dry

1 onion, quartered

1. Combine the onion powder, white pepper, thyme, garlic powder, cayenne pepper, paprika, salt, and black pepper in a bowl.

2. Rub the whole chicken with the powder mixture on all sides. Arrange the onion quarters into the cavity of the chicken.

3. Wrap the chicken with two layers of plastic and refrigerate for at least 4 hours.

4. Preheat the oven to 250ºF (120ºC).

5. Arrange the chicken in a baking pan and bake in the preheated oven for 5 hours or until a meat thermometer inserted in the center of the chicken reads at least 180ºF (82ºC).

6. Remove the chicken from the oven. Allow to cool for 10 minutes and slice to serve.

STORAGE: Store in an airtight container in the fridge for up to 4 days or in the freezer for up to 1 month.

REHEAT: Microwave, covered, until the desired temperature is reached or reheat in a frying pan or air fryer / instant pot, covered, on medium.

SERVE IT WITH: Easy lemon-ginger spinach is a perfect match for this dish, or you can have it with oven-roasted frozen broccoli cooked in the left juices. It will burst the flavors inside your mouth.

PER SERVING

calories: 484 | fat: 34.2g | total carbs: 2.2g | fiber: 0.6g | protein: 42.5g

27.Chicken Fajitas Bake

Macros: Fat 74% | Protein 21% | Carbs 5%

Prep time: 10 minutes | Cook time: 15 minutes | Serves 4 to 6

T his keto chicken casserole is the perfect low-carb meal for the

whole family. It has all of your favorite fajita flavors all in one

skillet. It is super simple, with only 7 main ingredients, and can be

made in about 20 minutes. This would be a great weeknight family-

friendly keto recipe. It's an easy keto recipe for beginners, too!

⅓ cup mayonnaise, keto-friendly 1 yellow onion, chopped

1 red bell pepper, chopped

1 rotisserie chicken breast, shred into bite-sized pieces

2 tablespoons Tex-Mex seasoning

2 tablespoons olive oil 5 ⅓ ounces (150 g) lettuce

7 ounces (198 g) cream cheese Salt and freshly ground black

pepper, to taste 7 ounces (198 g) shredded Cheddar cheese,

divided

1. Preheat the oven to 400°F (205°C).

2. Add all the ingredients except for a third of the cheese to a lightly greased casserole dish. Stir to combine well.

3. Top the mixture with remaining cheese, then arrange the casserole dish in the preheated oven. Bake for 15 minutes or until lightly browned.

4. Remove the casserole dish from the oven and serve warm.

STORAGE: Store in an airtight container in the fridge for up to 4 days.

REHEAT: Microwave, covered, until the desired temperature is reached or reheat in a frying pan or air fryer / instant pot, covered, on medium.

SERVE IT WITH: To make this a complete meal, you can serve this casserole dish with leafy greens dressed in olive oil.

PER SERVING

calories: 526 | fat: 43.1g | total carbs: 7.0g | fiber: 1.5g | protein: 27.7g

28.Savoury And Sticky Baked Chicken Wings

Macros: Fat 37% | Protein 62% | Carbs 1%

Prep time: 5 minutes | Cook time: 45 minutes | Serves 4

T hese wings are great. There is a heat to them, but non-spice lovers enjoy them too because of the sweetness. They have a sweet, spicy, smoky flavor that will make you do a happy dance for sure! Made with a keto-friendly homemade marinade you can ensure there's no nasty preservatives or refined sugars in these bad boys!

2 pounds (907 g) chicken wings

1 teaspoon sea salt

SAUCE:

¾ cup coconut aminos

¼ teaspoon garlic powder

¼ teaspoon red pepper flakes

¼ teaspoon onion powder

¼ teaspoon ground ginger

1. Preheat oven to 450°F (235°C).

2. Arrange the chicken wings in a baking pan, skin side down. Make sure to keep a little distance between wings.

3. Sprinkle salt to season the wings, then bake in the preheated oven for 45 minutes or until crispy and cooked through.

4. Meanwhile, make the sauce: Warm a nonstick skillet over medium heat, then add the coconut aminos, garlic powder, red pepper flakes, onion powder, and ginger powder. Bring them to a simmer.

5. Reduce the heat to low and keep simmering. Stir the mixture constantly to combine well until the sauce is lightly thickened.

6. Arrange the chicken wings on a large serving dish. Pour the sauce over to coat the chicken wings and serve warm.

STORAGE: Store in an airtight container in the fridge for up to 4 days.

REHEAT: Microwave, covered, until the desired temperature is reached or reheat in a frying pan or air fryer / instant pot, covered, on medium.

SERVE IT WITH: Serve them with roasted Brussels sprout and rich cod fish soup.

PER SERVING

calories: 450 | fat: 18.5g | total carbs: 9.4g | fiber: 0.1g | protein: 69.2g

29.Low-Carb Chicken With Tricolore Roasted Veggies

Macros: Fat 71% | Protein 21% | Carbs 8%

Prep time: 15 minutes | Cook time: 30 minutes | Serves 8

I t really is a beautiful and most colorful dish. So easy-to-make with lots of good flavor, and you can choose to cook it with either a whole chicken or chicken breasts.

TRICOLORE ROASTED VEGGIES:

8 ounces (227 g) mushrooms

1 pound (454 g) Brussels sprouts

8 ounces (227 g) cherry tomatoes

1 teaspoon dried rosemary

1 teaspoon sea salt

½ teaspoon ground black pepper ½ cup olive oil

FRIED CHICKEN:

4 chicken breasts

1 ounce (28 g) butter, for frying

Salt and freshly ground black pepper, to taste

4 ounces (113 g) herb butter, for serving

1. Preheat the oven to 400°F (205°C).

2. Arrange the mushrooms, Brussels sprouts, and cherry tomatoes in a baking pan.

3. Sprinkle with rosemary, salt, and ground black pepper. Pour the olive oil over. Stir to coat the veggies well.

4. Arrange the baking pan in the preheated oven and bake for about 20 minutes or until the Brussels spouts are wilted and the veggies are soft.

5. In the meantime, melt the butter in a nonstick skillet over medium heat, then place the chicken breasts in the pan. Sprinkle with salt and pepper.

6. Fry the chicken in the skillet for 8 to 10 minutes or until there is no pink on the chicken and the juices run clear.

7. Remove the baked veggies from the oven and serve with th e fried chicken.

STORAGE: Roasted vegetables can be stored in the refrigerator for 3 to 4 days. Store any leftover chicken in the fridge. This will store for up to three days.

REHEAT: Heat roasted vegetables again in a hot oven to keep them firm and crisp. A microwave will just turn them to mush. Spread the vegetables out on a baking sheet, drizzle them with olive oil, and bake at 450ºF (235ºC) for 4 or 5 minutes.

SERVE IT WITH: To make this a complete meal, you can serve it with with roasted Brussels sprout and rich sea white fish soup.

PER SERVING

calories: 390 | fat: 30.8g | total carbs: 10.4g | fiber: 3.1g | protein: 20.9g

Pork Recipes

30.Citrus Pork with Cabbage & Tomatoes

<u>Ingredients</u> for 2 servings

3 tbsp olive oil

2 tbsp lemon juice

1 garlic clove, pureed

2 pork loin chops

1/3 head cabbage, shredded

1 tomato, chopped

1 tbsp white wine

Salt & black pepper to taste

¼ tsp cumin

¼ tsp ground nutmeg

1 tbsp parsley

<u>Instructions - Total Time</u>: around 27 minutes

In a bowl, mix the lemon juice, garlic, salt, pepper and olive oil.

Brush the pork with the mixture. Preheat grill to high heat. Grill the

pork for 2-3 minutes on each side until cooked through. Remove to

serving plates. Warm the remaining olive oil in a pan and cook in cabbage for 5 minutes. Drizzle with white wine, sprinkle with cumin, nutmeg, salt and pepper. Add in the tomatoes, cook for another 5 minutes, stirring occasionally. Ladle the sautéed cabbage to the side of the chops and serve sprinkled with parsley.

Per serving: Cal 565; Fat 36.7g; Net Carbs 6.1g; Protein 43g

31. Pork Kofte with Tomato Passata & Basil

Ingredients for 2 servings

½ lb ground pork

1 tbsp olive oil

1 tbsp parsley, chopped

1 tbsp pork rinds, crushed

½ cup tomato sauce, sugar-free

1 garlic clove, minced

½ tsp oregano

1 shallot, chopped

1/3 cup Italian blend kinds of cheeses

1 small egg

1/3 tsp paprika

1 tbsp basil, chopped to garnish

Salt and black pepper to taste

Instructions - Total Time: around 45 minutes

In a bowl, mix the ground pork, shallot, pork rinds, garlic, egg, paprika, oregano, parsley, salt, and black pepper, just until combined. Form balls of the mixture and place them in an oiled baking pan; drizzle with olive oil. Bake in the oven for 18 minutes at 390 F. Pour the tomato sauce all over the meatballs. Sprinkle with the Italian blend cheeses, and put it back in the oven to bake for 10-15 minutes until the cheese melts. Once ready, take out the pan and garnish with basil. Delicious when served with cauliflower mash.

Per serving: Cal 586; Fat 38g; Net Carbs 7.3g; Protein 39.2g

32. Green Chimichurri Sauce with Grilled Pork Steaks

<u>**Ingredients**</u> for 2 servings

1 garlic clove, minced

2 tbsp extra-virgin olive oil

½ tsp white wine vinegar

8 oz pork loin steaks

2 tbsp parsley leaves, chopped

Salt and black pepper to season

2 tbsp cilantro leaves, chopped

2 tbsp sesame oil

<u>**Instructions - Total Time**</u>: around 64 minutes

To make the sauce: in a bowl, mix the parsley, cilantro and garlic. Add the vinegar, extra-virgin olive oil, and salt, and combine well. Preheat a grill pan over medium heat. Rub the pork with sesame oil, and season with salt and pepper. Grill the meat for 4-5 minutes on each side until no longer pink in the center. Put the pork on a serving plate and spoon chimichurri sauce over, to serve.

Per serving: Cal 452; Fat 33.6g; Net Carbs 2.3g; Protein 32.8g

33. Leek & Bacon Gratin

Ingredients for 4 servings

1 lb leeks, trimmed and sliced

1 tomato, chopped

3 oz bacon, chopped

2 tbsp water

2 cups baby spinach

1 cup grated mozzarella

4 oz halloumi cheese, cut into cheese

cubes

½ tsp dried oregano

2 garlic cloves, minced

Salt and black pepper to taste

1 cup buttermilk

Instructions - Total Time: around 35 minutes

Place a cast iron pan over medium heat and fry the bacon for 4 minutes, then add garlic and leeks and cook for 5-6 minutes. Preheat oven to 370 F. In a bowl, mix the buttermilk, tomato, and water, and add to the pan. Stir in the spinach, halloumi, oregano, salt, and pepper to taste. Sprinkle the mozzarella cheese on top and transfer the pan to the oven. Bake for 20 minutes or until the

cheese is golden. When ready, remove and serve the gratin.

Per serving: Cal 350; Fat 27g; Net Carbs 5.3g; Protein 16g

34. Cheese Stuffing Pork Rolls with Bacon

Ingredients for 2 servings

1 tbsp olive oil

1 spring onion, chopped

2 oz bacon, sliced

1 garlic clove, minced

1 tbsp fresh parsley, chopped

1 tbsp Parmesan cheese, grated

2 pork chops, boneless and flatten

5 oz canned diced tomatoes

¼ cup ricotta cheese

Salt & black pepper to taste

1 tbsp pine nuts

½ tsp herbes de Provence

Instructions - Total Time: around 40 minutes

Put the pork chops on a flat surface. Set the bacon slices on top, then divide the ricotta cheese, pine nuts, and Parmesan cheese. Roll each pork piece and secure with a toothpick. Set a pan over medium heat and warm oil. Cook the pork rolls until browned, and remove to a plate. Add in the spring onion and garlic, and cook for 5 minutes. Place in the stock and cook for 3 minutes. Get rid of the toothpicks

from the rolls and return them to the pan. Stir in the black pepper, salt, tomatoes and herbes de Provence. Bring to a boil, set heat to medium-low, and cook for 20 minutes while covered. Sprinkle with parsley to serve.

Per serving: Cal 631; Fat 42g; Net Carbs 7.1g; Protein 44g

Beef Recipes

35.Eggplant Beef Lasagn a

Ingredients **for 4 servings**

2 large eggplants, sliced lengthwise

2 tbsp olive oil

½ red chili, chopped

1 lb ground beef

2 garlic cloves, minced

1 shallot, chopped

1 cup tomato sauce

Salt and black pepper to taste

2 tsp sweet paprika

1 tsp dried thyme

1 tsp dried basil

1 cup mozzarella cheese, grated

1 cup chicken broth

Directions **and Total Time: approx. 65 minutes**

Heat the oil in a skillet and cook the beef for 4 minutes while breaking any lumps as you stir. Top with shallot, garlic, chili, tomato sauce, salt, paprika and black pepper. Stir and cook for 5 more minutes.

Lay 1/3 of the eggplant slices in a greased baking dish. Top with 1/3 of the beef mixture and repeat the layering process two more times with the same quantities. Season with basil and thyme. Pour in the chicken broth. Sprinkle the mozzarella cheese on top and tuck the baking dish in the oven. Bake for 35 minutes at 380 F. Remove the lasagna and let it rest for 10 minutes before serving.

Per serving: Cal 388; Fat 16g; Net Carbs 9.8g; Protein 41g

36.Beef Steaks with Bacon & Mushroom s

Ingredients **for 2 servings**

2 oz bacon, chopped

1 cup mushrooms, sliced

1 garlic clove, chopped

1 shallot, chopped

1 cup heavy cream

½ lb beef steaks

1 tsp ground nutmeg

¼ cup coconut oil

Salt and black pepper to taste

1 tbsp parsley, chopped

Directions **and Total Time: approx. 50 minutes**

In a pan over medium heat, cook the bacon for 2-3 minutes; set aside. In the same pan, warm the oil, add in the shallot, garlic and mushrooms. Cook for 4 minutes .

Stir in the beef, season with salt, pepper, and nutmeg, and sear until browned, 2 minutes per side.

Preheat oven to 360 F and insert the pan in the oven to bake for 25 minutes. Remove the beef steaks to a bowl and cover with foil. Place the pan over medium heat, pour in the heavy cream over the mushroom mixture, add in the reserved bacon and cook for 5 minutes; remove from heat. Spread the bacon/mushroom sauce over beef steaks, sprinkle with parsley and serve.

Per serving: Cal 765; Fat 71g; Net Carbs 3.8g; Protein 32g

37.Veggie Chuck Roast Beef in Ove n

Ingredients **for 4 servings**

2 tbsp olive oil

1 lb beef chuck roast, cubed

1 cup canned diced tomatoes

1 carrot, chopped

Salt and black pepper to taste

½ lb mushrooms, sliced

1 celery stalk, chopped

1 bell pepper, sliced

1 onion, chopped

1 bay leaf

½ cup beef stock

1 tbsp rosemary, chopped

½ tsp dry mustard

1 tbsp almond flour

<u>Directions</u> **and Total Time: approx. 1 hour 45 minutes**

Preheat oven to 350 F. Set a pot over medium heat, warm olive oil and brown the beef on each side for 4-5 minutes. Stir in tomatoes, onion, mustard, carrot, mushrooms, bell pepper, celery, bay leaf, and stock. Season with salt and pepper. In a bowl, combine ½ cup of water with flour and stir in the pot. Transfer to a baking dish and bake for 90 minutes, stirring at intervals of 30 minutes. Scatter the rosemary over and serve warm.

Per serving: Cal 325; Fat 18g; Net Carbs 5.6g; Protein 31g

38.Winter Beef Ste w

Ingredients **for 4 servings**

14 oz canned tomatoes with juice

3 tsp olive oil

1 lb ground beef

1 cup beef stock

1 carrot, chopped

1 celery stick, chopped

1 lb butternut squash, diced

1 tbsp Worcestershire sauce

2 bay leaves

Salt and black pepper to taste

3 tbsp fresh parsley, chopped

1 onion, chopped

1 tsp dried sage

1 garlic clove, minced

Directions and Total Time: approx. 40 minutes

Cook the onion, garlic, celery, carrot, and beef, in warm oil over medium heat for 10 minutes. Add in butternut squash, Worcestershire sauce, bay leaves, stock, canned tomatoes, and sage, and bring to a boil. Reduce heat and simmer for 20 minutes. Adjust the seasonings. Remove and discard the bay leaves. Serve topped with parsley.

Per serving: Cal 353; Fat 16g; Net Carbs 6.6g; Protein 26g

39.Beef Cheese & Egg Casserol e

Ingredients **for 4 servings**

2 tbsp olive oil

½ tsp nutmeg

1 lb ground beef

5 eggs, beaten

1 cup Gouda cheese, grated

1 yellow onion, chopped

2 cups tomatoes, chopped

¼ cup heavy cream 1 Banana pepper, chopped

2 garlic cloves, chopped 2 zucchinis, sliced

Salt and black pepper to taste

Directions **and Total Time: approx. 25 minutes**

Preheat oven to 360 F. Warm the olive oil in a skillet over medium heat. Stir-fry the garlic, banana pepper, and onion for 2 minutes until tender. Add the ground beef and sauté for 4-6 minutes, stirring often.

Sprinkle with nutmeg, salt, and pepper. Transfer the mixture to a baking dish. Cover with tomatoes and arrange the zucchini slices on top. Bake for 30 minutes.

In a bowl, mix the eggs, cheese, and heavy cream. Season with salt and pepper. Remove the baking dish from the oven and pour the cheese mixture over. Bake for 10-15 more minutes or until the eggs are set. Enjoy!

Per serving: Cal 608; Net Carbs 8.4g; Fat 36g; Protein 56g

Seafood Recipes

40.Tilapia with Olives & Tomato Sauce

Preparation Time: **10 minutes**

Cooking time: **50 minutes**

Servings **: 6**

Ingredients

- 4 tilapia fillets

- 2 garlic cloves, minced

- 2 tsp oregano

- 14 ounces diced tomatoes 1 tbsp olive oil

- ½ red onion, chopped 2 tbsp parsley

- **¼ cup kalamata olives**

Directions

1. Heat olive oil in a skillet over medium heat and cook the onion for 3 minutes.

2. Add garlic and oregano and cook for 30 seconds. Stir in tomatoes and bring the mixture to a boil. Reduce the heat and simmer for 5 minutes.

3. Add olives and tilapia and cook for about 8 minutes.

4. **Serve the tilapia with tomato sauce.**

Nutrition:

- Calories 66

- Fat 3.3 g

- Carbohydrates 9.9 g

- Sugar 5.1 g

- Protein 0.8 g

- Cholesterol 9 mg

41.Lemon Garlic Shrimp

Preparation Time: **10 minutes**

Cooking time : 50 minutes

Servings **: 6**

Ingredients

- ½ cup butter, divided

- 2 lb. shrimp, peeled and deveined

- Salt and black pepper to taste

- ¼ tsp sweet paprika

- 1 tbsp minced garlic 3 tbsp water

- 1 lemon, zested and juiced

- **2 tbsp chopped parsley**

Directions

1. Melt half of the butter in a large skillet over medium heat, season the shrimp with salt, black pepper, paprika, and add to the butter.

2. Stir in the garlic and cook the shrimp for 4 minutes on both sides until pink. Remove to a bowl and set aside.
3. Put the remaining butter in the skillet; include the lemon zest, juice, and water.
4. Add the shrimp, parsley, and adjust the taste with salt and pepper.
5. Cook for 2 minutes.
6. **Serve shrimp and sauce with squash pasta.**

Nutrition:

- Calories 245
- Fat 7.5 g
- Carbohydrates 32.8 g
- Sugar 3.5 g
- Protein 11.8 g
- Cholesterol 22 mg

Smoothies

42.Grilled Tofu Kabobs with Arugula Sala d

- <u>Ingredients</u> **for 4 servings**

- 14 oz firm tofu, cut into strips

- 4 tsp sesame oil

- 1 lemon, juiced

- 5 tbsp soy sauce, sugar-free

- 3 tsp garlic powder

- 4 tbsp coconut flour

- ½ cup sesame seeds

- Arugula salad

- 4 cups arugula, chopped

- 2 tsp extra virgin olive oil

- 2 tbsp pine nuts

- Salt and black pepper to taste

- 1 tbsp balsamic vinegar

- <u>Directions</u> **and Total Time: approx. 30 min + chilling time**

- Stick the tofu strips on the skewers, height-wise, and place them onto a plate. In a bowl, mix sesame oil, lemon juice, soy sauce, garlic powder, and coconut flour. Pour the soy sauce mixture over the tofu and turn in the sauce to coat. Cover the dish and place in the fridge for 2 hours.

- Heat the griddle pan over high heat. Rool the tofu in the sesame seeds and grill until golden brown on both sides, about 12 minutes in total. Arrange the arugula on a serving plate. Drizzle over olive oil and balsamic vinegar and season with salt and black pepper. Sprinkle with pine nuts and place the tofu kabobs on top to serve.

- **Per serving:** Cal 411; Fat 33g; Net Carbs 7.1g; Protein 22g

43.Steamed Bok Choy with Thyme & Garli c

- <u>Ingredients</u> **for 4 servings**

- 2 lb Bok choy, sliced 2 tbsp coconut oil

- 2 tbsp soy sauce, sugar-free

- 1 tsp garlic, minced ½ tsp thyme, chopped

- ½ tsp red pepper flakes

- Salt and black pepper to taste

- <u>Directions</u> **and Total Time: approx. 15 minutes**

- Place a pan over medium heat and warm the coconut oil. Add in garlic and cook until soft, 1 minute. Stir in the bok choy, red pepper, soy sauce, black pepper, salt, and thyme and cook until everything is heated through, about 5 minutes. Serve.

- **Per serving:** Cal 132; Fat 9.5g; Net Carbs 3.5g; Protein 4.9g

44.Sticky Tofu with Cucumber & Tomato Sala d

- Ingredients **for 4 servings**

- 2 tbsp olive oil

- 12 oz tofu, sliced

- 1 cup green onions, chopped

- 1 garlic clove, minced

- 2 tbsp vinegar 1 tbsp sriracha sauc e

- Salad 1 tbsp fresh lemon juice

- 2 tbsp extra virgin olive oil

- Salt and black pepper to taste

- 1 tsp fresh dill weed 1 cucumber, sliced

- 2 tomatoes, sliced

- Directions **and Total Time: approx. 15 min + chilling time**

- Put tofu slices, garlic, sriracha sauce, vinegar, and green onions in a bowl; allow to settle for approximately 30 minutes. Warm the olive oil in a skillet over medium heat. Cook tofu for 5 minutes until golden brown. In a salad plate, arrange tomatoes and cucumber slices, season with salt and pepper, drizzle lemon juice and extra virgin olive oil, and scatter dill all over. Top with the tofu and serve.

- **Per serving:** Cal 371; Fat 31g; Net Carbs 7.7g; Protein 17g

45.Grilled Vegetables & Tempeh Shish Keba b

- Ingredients **for 4 servings**

- 1 yellow bell pepper, cut into chunks

- 1 cup barbecue sauce, sugar-free

- 2 tbsp olive oil

- 10 oz tempeh, cut into chunks

- 1 red onion, cut into chunks

- 1 red bell pepper, cut chunks

- 1 cup zucchini, sliced

- 2 tbsp chives

- Directions **and Total Time: approx. 30 min + chilling time**

- In a pot over medium heat, pour 2 cups of water. Bring to boil, remove from heat and add the tempeh. Cover the pot and let tempeh steam for 5 minutes to remove its bitterness. Drain the tempeh. Pour the barbecue sauce into a bowl, add the tempeh to it, and coat with the sauce. Cover the bowl and marinate in the fridge for 2 hours.

- Preheat grill to medium heat. Thread the tempeh, yellow bell pepper, red bell pepper, zucchini, and onion.

- Brush the grate of the grill with olive oil, place the skewers on it, and brush with barbecue sauce. Cook the skewers for 3 minutes on each side while rotating and brushing with more barbecue sauce. Once ready, transfer the kabobs to a plate and serve sprinkled with chives.

- **Per serving:** Cal 228; Fat 15g; Net Carbs 3.6g; Protein 13g

Sweets & Desserts Recipes

46.Mascarpone Cream Mousse

Ingredients for 6 servings

For the mascarpone	*For the vanilla mousse*
8 oz heavy cream	3.5 oz heavy cream
8 oz mascarpone cheese	3.5 oz cream cheese
4 tbsp cocoa powder	1 tsp vanilla extract
4 tbsp xylitol	2 tbsp xylitol

- **Instructions - Total Time**: around 15 minutes

- In a bowl, using an electric mixer, beat mascarpone cheese, heavy cream, cocoa powder, and xylitol until creamy. Do not over mix, however. In another bowl, whisk all the

- mousse ingredients until smooth and creamy. Gradually fold vanilla mousse mixture into the mascarpone one

until well incorporated. Spoon into dessert cups and
serve.

- **Per serving**: Cal 409; Net Carbs 5.9g; Fat 32g; Protein
  7.9g

47. Chocolate Mousse Pots with Blackberries

Ingredients for 4 servings

2 ½ cups unsweetened dark chocolate, melted

½ cup swerve confectioner's sugar

3 cups heavy cream

½ tsp vanilla extract

½ cup blackberries, chopped

Some blackberries for topping

- **Instructions - Total Time**: around 10 min + chilling time

- In a stand mixer, beat heavy cream and swerve sugar until creamy. Add dark chocolate and vanilla extract and mix until smoothly combined. Fold in blackberries until well distributed. Divide the mixture between 4 dessert cups, cover with plastic wrap, and refrigerate for 2 hours. Garnish with the reserved blackberries and serve.

- **Per serving**: Cal 309; Net Carbs 2.6g; Fat 33g; Protein 2g

48. Mojito Mousse with Blackberries

<u>Ingredients</u> for 4 servings

2 ½ cups sour cream

Chopped mint to garnish

3 cups heavy cream

½ cup swerve confectioner's sugar

3 limes, juiced

12 blackberries for topping

½ tsp vanilla extract

- **Instructions - Total Time**: around 10 min + chilling time

- In a stand mixer, beat heavy cream and swerve sugar until creamy. Add sour cream, lime juice, and vanilla; combine smoothly. Divide between 4 dessert cups, cover with plastic wrap, and refrigerate for 2 hours. Remove, garnish with mint leaves, top with blackberries, and serve.

- **Per serving**: Cal 489; Net Carbs 8.7g; Fat 43g; Protein 3.9g

49.Avocado Mousse with Chocolate

Ingredients for 4 servings

1 avocado, pitted & peeled

1 heaped tbsp cocoa powder

2 tbsp cream of tartar

1 cup Greek yogurt

1 cup full fat coconut cream

- **Instructions - Total Time**: around 10 min + chilling time

- In a food processor, add coconut cream, avocado, cocoa powder, cream of tartar, and Greek yogurt. Blend until smooth. Divide the mixture between 4 dessert cups and chill in the refrigerator for at least 2 hours. Serve.

- **Per serving**: Cal 329; Net Carbs 8.2g; Fat 31g; Protein 6g

50. Chocolate Mocha Mousse Cups

Ingredients for 4 servings

2 tbsp butter, softened

8 oz cream cheese, softened

2/3 cup heavy whipping cream

3 tbsp sour cream

1 ½ tsp vanilla extract

1/3 cup erythritol

3 tsp instant coffee powder

¼ cup cocoa powder

1 ½ tsp swerve sugar

½ tsp vanilla extract

- **Instructions - Total Time**: around 10 minutes

- In a bowl, using an electric hand mixer, beat cream cheese, sour cream, and butter until smooth. Mix in vanilla, erythritol, coffee and cocoa powders until incorporated. In a separate bowl, beat whipping cream until soft peaks form. Mix in swerve sugar and vanilla until well combined. Fold 1/3 of the whipped cream mixture into the cream cheese mixture to lighten a bit.

Fold in the remaining mixture until well incorporated.

Spoon into dessert cups.

- **Per serving**: Cal 310; Net Carbs 4g; Fat 29g; Protein 5g

CONCLUSION

- ongratulations for making it this far! By now, I trust you already have a good understanding of the Ketogenic Diet and how it applies to you as you enjoy your 50s. Obviously, our goal here is to provide a Keto Diet guideline that works for you, taking into account your unique situation so that the best and most effective results can be achieved.

- The ketogenic diet is one that has many important aspects and information that you need to know as someone who wants to try this diet. It is important to remember the warning that we have given you at the beginning of the book that this is not a diet that is safe and that doctors don't recommend to try it, and if you are going to attempt it remember that you shouldn't do so for longer than six months and even then never without the constant supervision of a doctor or at the very least a doctor knowing that you're doing this and that you're following their guidelines and words to the letter so they can make sure you are safe.

- The ketogenic diet is a diet that believes that by minimizing your carbs while maximizing the good fat in your system while making sure that you're getting the protein you need; you will be happier and healthier. In this guidebook, we give you the information to know what this diet is all about, as well as describing the different types and areas that this diet will offer. Most people assume that there is only one way to do this and while there is one thing that the additional options share, there are four different options you can choose from. Each one has its unique benefits, and you should know about each type to learn what would be best for your body, which is why we have described them in the book for you to have the best information possible when you begin this diet for yourself.

- Another important thing about this diet is that many people don't understand the importance of exercise with this diet. The best way to become healthier is to do three things for yourself. Get the right amount of sleep, eat healthily, and make sure that you get the proper amount of exercise as well for your body to work at an optimum level. The exercises, such as the ones that we explained, are the best to go with your diet to make sure that you are getting the most out of it.

- For women who are on the go and have a busy lifestyle, we have provided recipes for a thirty-day meal plan so that you can make food quickly and have a great meal for their lifestyles. They also have enough servings for you to have leftovers so that you don't have to worry about preparing more food in the morning. Instead, you can simply pack it up and take it with you wherever you go. This works out so much easier for so many people because they don't have to cook in the morning, and it saves a busy person a lot of time.

- With all this information at your fingertips, you will be able to enjoy this diet and use it to your advantage. Another benefit that we offer is that we explain routines that you can do for yourself to make this diet last longer for you and to benefit your body better as a result. Routines are very important and can be a big help to your body but also your spirit and your mind. Good luck with your keto journey!

- One of the easiest ways to stay on your plan is to minimize the temptations. Remove the chocolate, candy, bread, pasta, rice, and sugary sodas you have supplied in your kitchen. If you live alone, this is an easy task. It is a bit more challenging if you have a family. The diet will also be useful for them if you plan your meals using the recipes included in this book.

- If you cheat, that must count also. It will be a reminder of your indulgence, but it will help keep you in line. Others may believe you are obsessed with the plan, but it is your health and wellbeing that you are improving .

- When you go shopping for your ketogenic essentials be sure you take your new skills, a grocery list, and search the labels. Almost every food item in today's grocery store has a nutrition label. Be sure you read each of the ingredients to discover any hiding carbs to keep your ketosis in line. You will be glad you took the extra time.

- One significant motivation behind why we get so disappointed with standard weight control plans is that they regularly become misjudged and accomplish more damage than anything else.

- So, in case you're needing a little motivation to read the book again, simply don't be excessively hard on yourself on the off chance that you miss a class or enjoy somewhat more than you needed. With these statements, you will realize that disappointment is part to remember the procedure.

- But I think the most important thing I want you to learn from this book is this: it's never too late to make that change! It's never too late to try something new for self-improvement !

CPSIA information can be obtained
at www.ICGtesting.com
Printed in the USA
LVHW060815260521
688043LV00037B/446